Booklets by Charlotte Gerson:
- Healing "Auto-Immune" Diseases
- Healing Brain & Kidney Cancer the Gerson Way
- Healing Breast Cancer the Gerson Way
- Healing Colon, Liver & Pancreatic Cancer the Gerson Way
- Healing Lung Cancer & Respiratory Diseases the Gerson Way
- Healing Lymphoma the Gerson Way
- Healing Melanoma the Gerson Way
- Healing Ovarian & Female Organ Cancer the Gerson Way
- Healing Prostate & Testicular Cancer the Gerson Way

MW00849494

Gerson Health Media
316 Mid Valley Center #230, Carmel, CA 93923
(831) 625-3565 | info@gersonmedia.com | www.gersonmedia.com

The Gerson Institute
P.O. Box 161358, San Diego, CA 92176
(619) 685-5353 | Fax: (619) 685-5363
Toll Free in US (888) 4-GERSON (4437766)
info@gerson.org | www.gerson.org

Acknowledgements

The author gratefully acknowledges the tireless and dedicated assistance of both Beata Bishop for her able editing of the materials, and Howard Straus for the mechanical work involved in turning words into published material. Without their help, the production of these booklets would have been far more difficult and time-consuming. But the real heroes, and the people without whom these booklets would be impossible are the patients and companions who did the day-to-day kitchen work associated with healing these diseases. We are deeply indebted to them for permission to use their inspiring stories. These booklets were prepared under the auspices of the Cancer Research Wellness Network, with generous grants from Mrs. Faye Joseph, Sting and Mrs. Trudie Styler.

This booklet, one of a series, lays no claim to being a scientific document. What it aims to do is to present, through a number of factual case histories, a novel approach to cancer and other chronic degenerative diseases that is totally different from the present-day philosophy and practice of orthodox medicine.

This approach, the Gerson Therapy®, has been practiced successfully for over sixty years, often achieving healing in so-called incurable cases where all else had failed. Yet until very recently it existed in relative obscurity. It is only now, when the limitations of modern high-technology medicine have become painfully obvious, that the potential of a truly holistic, scientifically sound medical modality is attracting growing interest.

What the Gerson Therapy lacks at present is the kind of large-scale research material, yielding a significant amount of statistics, without which its claims will not be accepted by the medical and/or academic Establishment. The reasons for this lack are simple. After Dr Gerson's death in 1959 the therapy was not practiced anywhere, right until 1977 when it was re-activated by Charlotte Gerson and several physicians in a newly established clinic in Mexico. In those early days the only aim was to help as many desperate patients as possible. Although naturally precise records were kept, embarking on a systematic research program was not feasible.

Years later, with the therapy running smoothly and attracting growing interest, another obstacle to research has become evident. Patients arrive from all parts of the world to a Gerson® facility in Mexico and after a few weeks return home, where they are supposed to remain on the therapy for a minimum of two years. In order to compile the results of the treatment in a statistically meaningful form, it would be necessary to follow up individual patients scattered all over the globe, monitor their progress, assess their success or failure, and obtain full medical documentation of each case.

The non-profit Gerson Institute has never had the funds or the manpower to carry out this expensive operation. Clearly, this puts it at a disadvantage from the orthodox medical point of view, which puts a high value on statistics and on randomized double blind clinical trials. The latter are suitable for testing a single new drug or treatment modality, but not a complex, many-faceted system of healing whose every component interacts with all the others. Until this basic difference is recognized by the critics of the therapy, it will be impossible to engage in a meaningful dialogue.

Hence the present series of booklets contains no statistics. What it offers instead is a number of authentic case histories, chosen from a large amount of clinical material. They tell the full, factual human stories of individuals confronted with life-threatening disease and overcoming it on an unorthodox therapy. Their stories may be dismissed by the strictly scientifically-minded as anecdotal evidence, but unless the lessons of such individual experiences are properly evaluated, there can be no hope of true progress in modern medicine's fight against today's killer diseases. Yet progress is badly needed, since some other sets of statistics, those of cancer mortality and of the rising tide of new cases, show no sign of improvement. It is time for conventional medicine to search for new paths of healing, and that is what the Gerson Therapy has to offer.

Introduction

In his last book, the classic work on the Gerson Therapy,
Dr. Gerson states his understanding of the origins of cancer:

> "In my opinion, cancer is not a problem of deficiencies of
> hormones, vitamins and enzymes. It is not a problem of
> allergies or infections, viral or others; it is not a poisoning
> through some metabolic of external substance (carcinogen),
> nor caused by a genetic factor. It is an accumulation of
> numerous damaging factors, in combination causing the
> deterioration of the entire metabolism when the liver has
> been progressively impaired."

In other words, it is a mistake to search for "THE cause of
cancer." There is no one single cause. With metabolic healing by
the Gerson Therapy, it has been our experience that even presum-
ably genetic cancers can be cured. The genes may well predispose
the person to weakness of the liver and/or the immune system. But
the damage is reversible!

When persons learn about metabolic, nutritional healing and
the Gerson Therapy, they often inquire about other patients who
were diagnosed with the same problem as the one from which
they are suffering, and ask whether the Gerson Therapy has
proved effective in such cases. In order to reassure such patients,
we have prepared the present booklet containing many reports of
recoveries in such specific cases.

Ovarian cancer is generally rather aggressive, more so in
younger women. And, according to the tenets of orthodox medicine, it has to be "treated aggressively." If this were to bring
long-term recoveries, it would be welcome. However, surgery,
radiation and large doses of chemotherapy produce at best only
temporary results. When the tumors recur, orthodox medicine is
helpless. The more recent, and among the most toxic types of
chemotherapy, Taxol, and the somewhat modified, Taxotere, also
only produce temporary, if any, positive results, but have
extremely toxic side effects.

A famous case in point is that of the beloved comedienne Gilda
Radner. In 1985, while filming *Movers and Shakers*, she suffered
from chronic fatigue and bouts of illness. Her doctors dismissed it
as "flu" or overwork. In 1986, she collapsed and was diagnosed

with advanced ovarian cancer. She went through nearly three years of chemotherapy, surgery and 30 radiation treatments. At one time she appeared on the cover of a national magazine, widely touted as being "in remission." Nevertheless, as almost all ovarian cancer patients, she died. She was 42. It was May of 1989.

As in all cancers, the problem is the breakdown of the body's systems and its normal defenses, including the immune system, the hormone system, the digestive tract and the vital organs (the liver, pancreas, heart, lungs, kidneys and spleen). As a result of this general breakdown, the organism is unable to absorb nutrients and adequately dispose of its natural wastes. At the same time it accumulates toxins from the air, water, soil, food, and environmental chemical sources, as well as from alcohol, smoking, and all drugs, whether medically prescribed, over-the-counter or "recreational." (Medical drugs suppress symptoms, but all are eventually liver-toxic. There are no exceptions.)

In order to truly heal the body, Dr Gerson found that two major actions were needed: to detoxify the body, and to flood it with the best natural nutrients. In other words, healing can only occur if the basic causes of the disease are reversed. Obviously, the ingestion and absorption of all toxins must also be avoided — a tall order in our toxic, polluted modern world. In several female cancers (ovarian, breast) the patient is tested for hormone levels, since orthodox medicine claims that certain cancers are 'hormone dependent.' In other words, if the patient has a high hormone level, this is supposed to stimulate more tumor growth. Interestingly, Dr. Gerson found that by detoxifying the liver (with coffee enemas), it is quite easy to help the liver to normalize the hormone levels, so that all hormone depressant drugs could be eliminated. All those drugs are carcinogenic and liver-toxic; therefore it is important to wean the patient off them.

It is not surprising that the basic causes are the same in all malignancies. Still, the primary affected area where the malignancy arises can be anywhere in the multitude of body tissues or organs! That is where other factors come into the picture: genetic weakness, long term irritation, recurrent infections, drug, alcohol and cigarette use, severe trauma, toxins (carcinogens), in soil, food, water and air. Even so, except in the most severe advanced cases, the malignancies are reversible.

To prove this claim, Dr Gerson — having exactly described the theory and practice of the therapy in his classic book, *A Cancer Therapy: Results of 50 Cases* — presented the thoroughly documented case histories of fifty recovered patients. All but two were in a terminal condition, having been sent home to die. All survived at least five years. Some who were young at the time when the book was published in 1958 are still alive and active nearly half a century later. In order to reassure current patients that people are still recovering from terminal cancers, (ovarian cancer in the present case), we are including in this booklet the stories of many recovered patients, cured of terminal disease and remaining well.

The Nutritional Healing Program of Max Gerson, M.D.

In order to help the body, with the liver as its major healing organ, to restore and heal, a number of life-style factors have to be radically changed. The first thing is the elimination of all animal proteins. This is a 'shocker' for most people who are trained and imbued with the idea that proteins (in their minds, animal-proteins) have to be part of their diet to promote normal health and tissue repair. More and more evidence is accumulating that the human body is not designed for and doesn't thrive on animal proteins. Our teeth, stomach acid level, long intestinal tract and more are all features of vegetarian animals. Further, more research now proves that the higher animal protein consumption, the higher chronic disease and cancer incidence. Dr. T. Colin Campbell, a professor in the division of Nutritional Sciences at Cornell University, and senior advisor to the American Institute for Cancer Research, said that there is

> "… a strong correlation between dietary protein intake and cancer of the breast, prostate, pancreas and colon." (as quoted in Lang, S., "Diet and Disease," *Food Monitor*, May/June 1983, p. 24)

Dr. Campbell recently (June '01) quoted additional research showing a clear relationship between cancer incidence and protein consumption in all cancers. He also showed graphs pointing to the fact that those patients who stopped all animal protein consumption had arrested their cancers or even occasionally caused them to be reduced.

Then comes the inevitable question, "But where will I get my proteins?" There are now many studies noted by Nathan Pritikin, John Robbins, and various US Government agencies, such as *The Journal of the American Dietetic Association* that clearly state that "A diet adequate to cover hunger, satisfied with natural foods, is more than adequate in proteins." I often simply ask the questioner to consider, "Where does the cow get her proteins?" and the answer is, of course, from grass.

The Gerson Nutritional Treatment is more than adequate in vegetarian proteins, so much so that it is capable of restoring and rebuilding organ systems, bones, and tissues ravaged by cancer.

The next problem of an average diet is the sodium (salt) intake.

Dr. Gerson was aware from the start of his experimenting with diet changes that salt was one of the main offenders of the metabolism. He found it hard to prove, except by what he considered the most important thing of all, the results at the sickbed. When patients came to his clinic, generally given up by their doctors and in terminal condition, he was able to reverse the disease. He found that one lady who didn't respond to his therapy at all, was only using salt to brush her teeth. (Presently, baking soda [sodium!] is recommended by doctors and dentists!). On discontinuing this practice, she showed good healing. It was only after Dr. Gerson's death in 1959 that researchers were able to study the damage caused by salt. Two scientists, Malcolm Dixon and Edwin C. Webb published their study in a book called *Enzymes*. Published by the Academic Press, Inc. New York 1964, 2nd Edition, pp. 422-423. In this table they show that as the body manufactures enzymes for all its needs, it uses potassium as its 'Activating Ion,' while in almost all cases, sodium (salt) was the enzyme inhibitor. "Poisons" are also defined as enzyme inhibitors. But Dr. Gerson did not have the facilities to do research of this type and went by the results he obtained. Salt in every form had to be totally banned from the patients' diet. This presents a problem with appetite at the start of the treatment. However, in about a week or two, the patient's taste buds become accustomed to the natural flavor of foods, spiced with fresh garlic, onion, celery and tomatoes instead of salt. Appetite returns.

The third damaging food item that has to be completely eliminated is fat. There is only one exception: straight, organic Flax Seed Oil (without any additions). ALL other fats and oils promote and stimulate tumor growth. They have been tried. Also, don't heat or cook with flax seed oil. Use this oil raw as in salad dressing or on baked potatoes once they are cool enough to eat.

The Gerson Therapy book gives many additional 'forbidden' items, such as white flour, sugar, alcohol, cigarettes, canned, frozen and pickled foods; cosmetics and underarm deodorants, household chemicals, sprays, pesticides and many more toxic and otherwise damaging materials. Also, all food and materials used for juices must be organically grown, free of poisons. Water must be cleared of fluorides (only possible with distilling) and other additives. If no fluoride is present, reverse osmosis will adequately clear the water. All water used for the patient, including that used in coffee enemas, must be clear of additives.

We come back to the original premise of all chronic disease and, of course, cancer patients. The problem is two-fold: Toxicity and Deficiency. Both must be addressed. Above all, we are dealing to some extent with preventing further toxins from entering the body. We not only have to be concerned with that situation; but we also have to detoxify the body of years of accumulated poisons and problems. That is accomplished with the coffee enemas.

A correct diet that doesn't burden the body with difficult-to-digest and toxic materials (animal proteins and fats; drugs, alcohol, etc., etc.) combined with the hourly freshly pressed juices, cause the cells and tissues to release these toxins — into the blood stream. The blood stream is filtered through the liver; it passes through the liver approximately once every three minutes. But there would be a huge overload on the liver if we didn't help it to eliminate this toxic burden. That is done via the coffee enemas. These have been shown to open bile ducts and allow the liver to clear itself not only of old accumulations but also of the tumor tissue that the body's immune system attacks and destroys. It is an ongoing process for many months. The patient may be surprised that it takes five such coffee enemas daily (once every four hours starting at 6 AM) to keep the liver clear. This procedure also overcomes pain in almost all cases, usually within the first two to three days of the Treatment.

The enemas are prepared as follows: Use a quart of 'clean' (distilled or filtered, see above) water; add three rounded table-spoonfuls of organic ground coffee (NOT de-caffeinated), bring to a boil and let simmer about 18 minutes. Let cool, strain, replace water that has evaporated to make up a full quart at body temperature; place into enema bucket or bag. Lie comfortably on a padded place or cot (or use your bed properly protected by a rubber or plastic sheet and towel) on your right side. Bucket or bag should not be much more than about 18 inches above your body so the flow is gentle. If possible, hold the coffee for no more than 12 minutes. If cramping or serious urgency is present, let it out when necessary. In time, 12 minutes will be quite easy.

Nutrition: In order to restore the depleted body systems, we have to use a form of 'hyper-alimentation'; *however,* **DON'T** use canned or processed products. *USE* only fresh, organic foods and juices. Thirteen 8-ounce glasses of freshly prepared juices are needed, one every hour starting at 7 or 8 AM. The correct kind of juicer (NOT a centrifugal type) is needed to get proper mineral extraction. One glass of orange juice, also freshly pressed, is given at breakfast; the other juices are five glasses of a mix of carrots and apples; three glasses of carrot juice only, four glasses of juice made from salad greens with one apple added per glass. This is NOT a juice fast. Three regular vegetarian, salt- and fat-free meals are given. All foods and juices are freshly prepared from organic fruit and vegetables. Juices are better digested with some solid meals, also cooked soup, potatoes and vegetables, and fruit (raw or stewed) for dessert.

Dr. Gerson became aware that patients are severely deficient in potassium, one of the most essential minerals. Potassium is amply present in all fruit, a little less so in vegetables. However, since the deficiency is so great, a potassium supplement of his own composition, is used. Also as part of the patient's medication, certain digestive enzymes are given, including pancreatic enzymes and a combination of stomach acid and pepsin, called "Acidolls." Liver medication, Vitamin B-3 and other items are also needed and given.

All foods, enema preparation, healing reactions, medication, and changes in the treatment required for patients pre-treated with chemotherapy drugs is described in great detail in the newly updated book, *Healing the Gerson Way: Defeating Cancer and Other Chronic Diseases.* (Available from Gerson Health Media, 316 Mid Valley Center #230, Carmel, CA 93923. Cost: $29.95, plus $4.00 shipping. California residents, add 8.5% sales tax.)

Most important of all: The Recovered Patients. These are reports by the patients of their experiences before the treatment and their overcoming of ovarian cancer. It is important to note that some (especially the first case described) suffered from multiple problems that were all cleared. The Gerson Nutritional Treatment is not specific for cancer, certainly not for just one form of cancer. When the treatment activates the body's "Healing

Mechanism" (as Dr. Gerson called it) it is impossible to selectively clear just one disease. Everything heals.

Leslie Tell — Ovarian Cancer

When Leslie was just 40, in March 1985, and because she was suffering from extreme fatigue, an ultrasound examination was performed. It showed a large abdominal mass. She had exploratory surgery, which resulted in a total hysterectomy, removal of her fallopian tubes, her omentum (the covering of the abdominal organs) plus the removal of all tumors larger than 1 cm in size. One of her ovarian tumors had split its capsule and seeded her entire abdominal cavity with metastases. They had spread to the peritoneal wall, the spleen, the diaphragm, the lower cecum (the start of the large intestine), the appendix, the rear pelvic wall, and the bladder wall. The small amount of fluid also present was filled with adenocarcinoma (malignant) cells. Her liver seemed clear. After the removal of all the tumors larger than 1 cm, a large number of smaller ones remained in the various abdominal organs.

Leslie called "her cancer" *Gilda Radner's cancer.* Some months into Leslie's Therapy, Life magazine carried a large article with Gilda on the cover, saying, "she has beaten cancer." This was 17 months into her [chemo] treatment. Leslie said, "I was pulling for her." However, when Gilda died, Leslie was very frightened since, "after all, she had the same disease as me. It's scary when somebody dies."

Leslie had a little seven-year old girl and wanted very much to live. After much mental agonizing, she decided to reject chemotherapy, which had little promise of recovery, and chose to do the Gerson Therapy. In the beginning she had very violent healing reactions, with pain all over her body.

On the fifth day of the Gerson Therapy, Leslie had a very high fever. "I just ached. I've never felt so terrible; it was like the worst case of flu that you can even imagine. Every joint, every part of my body was just aching. I also had killer headaches. I could hardly move. I was taking so many coffee enemas, one after another, just to give myself a little relief. Then, the next day, I started getting nausea. I took the green drink as a retention enema and drank copious amounts of peppermint tea and a little oatmeal gruel and some watermelon juice." Leslie goes on to report: "What was so phenomenal was that the onset of the healing reaction was just like throwing a light switch, it was that sudden. I felt fine one minute and deathly ill the next. And when it ended, it was just as sudden. I was taking a 'coffee break' and was still feeling just lousy. I got up and knew — it was over!"

Leslie reports that over a period of two years she had dozens of these reactions, never as strong again, nor ever with that high a fever again. After three years on the Gerson Therapy, Leslie's energy was high and she felt wonderful.

Leslie also consulted Dr. Nieper in Germany. He performed a CAT scan every time she visited for a follow up, in November of 1985, in June of 1987 and in June of 1989. Nothing positive was found at those times.

At this writing, in 2002, more than 17 years after her devastating diagnosis, and without chemotherapy, Leslie remains well and active and has good energy.

Diagnosis made at Orlando General Hospital, Inc., Orlando, Florida, on March 7 1985:

Bilateral primary papillary serous cystadenocarcinoma. Figo classification Stage III.

Sandra Whitwell — Ovarian Cancer

As a teenager, Sandra missed school at least one day a month, because her periods were so painful. At the age of 23, she had cysts the size of a grapefruit on her ovaries, ready to rupture. Emergency surgery removed the cysts. Because she had no children, no hysterectomy was done.

At age 29, Sandra developed endometriosis. Her tubes were scraped, but again a hysterectomy was not performed. Aged 37, Sandra had become an avid runner, running four to five miles a day. On a Wednesday she had run four miles, had absolutely no pain and no idea that anything was wrong with her. However, she awoke on Thursday morning with her stomach swollen, especially on the left side. She could not move, she was in such pain. Her doctor rushed her to the hospital and did emergency surgery. This time she was given a complete hysterectomy. She still had not birthed any children, but adoption has proven to be a blessed option. Two days after surgery, the lab results came back showing she had 'clear cell carcinoma of the ovaries.'

She was sent to Vanderbilt to see Dr. Jones, the oncologist, and chemotherapy was recommended. A friend living in Alaska sent Sandra information about the Gerson Therapy. Her mother had nursed a lot of people who had taken chemotherapy, and they decided it would be better to do nothing rather than chemo. They checked out macrobiotics and other options, but the Gerson Therapy made the most sense. Bombard the body with nutrients and it will recover and fight the cancer itself. Sandra decided to go to the Gerson Therapy clinic in Mexico, stayed 10 days, and her Mother and Dad literally devoted two years of their lives to her recovery — and the raising of her son.

Today Sandra feels better than she did when she was a teenager. She'd had lumps in her breast and one on her left leg. They've disappeared. When she first started the detoxification, she smelled of perms. She had always permed her hair, but now it is straight and healthy and her body no longer exudes that terrible smell. She also had terrible sinus problems and would vomit for days with migraine headaches, which no longer exist. She is presently helping a friend with ovarian cancer to do the Gerson Therapy, and is learning how hard her parents worked and are still working, as they are also helping. To Sandra the Gerson Therapy makes very much sense and has become a wonderful way of life for her. She adds, " It is hard socially, but I am a great conversation piece!"

Two years ago, Sandra had a terrible experience. After having a root canal done, she developed pain in the root canal tooth, pain in her neck, shoulders, knees and hips. Even her head seemed to be flipping and she became so nervous that her hands would shake. She kept telling the dentist that the tooth caused all this. She got laughs and plenty of explanations as to why this could not be so. She even developed a knot on her nose and left eyelid. After a visit to the dentist who did the root canal and four visits to her regular dentist, Sandra finally got the tooth pulled. Immediately her heart stopped flipping and the pain disappeared. She is still working on the cysts on her nose and eyelid. They have decreased greatly and are no longer obvious — but they are still there.

Mary Hildebrand — Ovarian Cancer

Mary Hildebrand had some intestinal discomfort for years, with "irritable bowel syndrome" causing alternating bouts of cramping and diarrhea as well as constipation. She also felt that she "wasn't digesting well."

In late summer of 1985, she was just returning from a European trip with camping and relaxation and actually felt well when she noticed some lumps in her lower pelvic area. She didn't suspect any serious problem and assumed these had something to do with her occasional bowel problems. However, the lumps "didn't go away," so Mary consulted a gynecologist. This doctor sent her for an ultrasound examination, which showed an orange-size mass on one ovary, while the other one had a mass the size of a grapefruit. Because of her age, (she was only 32), the doctor was "almost certain that this was not cancer, just some benign masses." Surgery was scheduled for September 25th, 1985. When Mary woke up after surgery to remove the masses, she found that she had been given a total hysterectomy. Further examination also revealed that she had some spreading to the periaortic lymph nodes, with the official diagnosis of "Grade I papillary serous carcinoma with spreading to the lymph node"

Obviously, with her ovaries removed, Mary was thrown into immediate menopause. This is serious at such a young age, and she suffered from the typical symptoms. While she was still recovering at the hospital from her surgery, a friend brought her Dr. Gerson's book, *A Cancer Therapy: Results of 50 Cases*. Her regular doctors had suggested one year of chemotherapy, but Mary just felt it wasn't right for her. Her doctors were appalled by the idea of alternative therapies. One doctor whom she consulted for a check-up didn't want to talk to her at all and demanded that she get out of his office! However, in spite of the vocal objections of her doctors, family and friends, she decided to go to the Mexican Gerson Hospital, where she arrived toward the middle of October 1985. She had originally planned to stay for two weeks; but actually stayed for three months. At about that time, some friends started to visit her in Mexico. When they saw how well Mary looked, they became less negative. Subsequently, she found a pleasant place down the coast of the Baja California peninsula, where she stayed for another six to seven months, with some hired help. Her husband picked up organic food and liver (liver juice was still being used at that time) and she now states that "she never missed one juice" during that time of close to one year on the full Gerson Therapy.

Meantime, her menopause symptoms were almost cleared on the Therapy. When she returned home, she went on a somewhat modified therapy, working with a Dr. B. for another three months, and then stayed on about three to five juices, weaned herself off enemas, worked with Carl Simonton, using bio-feedback and visualization. Mary also made personal and career changes. At the end of 1986, she was divorced and also went back to school to be a health therapist, becoming seriously involved with psycho-neuro-immunology. She is feeling very well (in mid-2001) and is taking very low dose HRT (Premarin and Provera).

Mary had an MRI in June of 1987. All masses were completely gone by that time.

Diagnosis made at Stanford University Hospital, Stanford, California, on October 11, 1985:

Ovaries, left and right, oophorectomy and hysterectomy — Grade I serous papillary carcinoma Lymph nodes, periaortic, biopsies – metastatic Grade I papillary serous carcinoma.

Barbara Conklin — Ovarian Cancer

Barbara was born in 1942 in Cincinnati, Ohio. Aged 7, she had polio that left her with scoliosis (abnormal curvature of the spine), and the need for a leg brace and crutches to enable her to walk. Later she went to college and graduated with a Master's degree in psychiatric social work. She married "a wonderful husband" who has always been supportive in whatever she wanted to do.

In 1983, suffering from allergies, she and her husband moved to Florida, and started following an organic vegetarian diet. She had been reading avidly about alternative medicine for 15 years.

In October 1995, she felt lumps in her abdominal area. Her gynecologist had an ultrasound done which showed two tumors, while a CA 125 test produced a score of 398 (a normal score is below 31). Barbara chose to have a complete hysterectomy, which was biopsied. The diagnosis was a very fast growing ovarian cancer, Stage II.

After surgery, her cancer score dropped to 85; after three weeks on the Gerson Therapy, it went down to 31. Since then the CA 125 has fluctuated from as low as 6 to 16. In January 1998, with the reduction of the intensive Therapy, the CA 125 was 11.

Following her operation, the surgeon advised Barbara to have chemotherapy. She refused. He told her that the prognosis for recovery from ovarian cancer after surgery and chemotherapy was 20%. Without chemotherapy it was approximately 2%. Since her odds for survival were very poor, Barbara contacted Charlotte Gerson and opted to go to the Gerson Hospital in Mexico. Since her prognosis was bad, she wanted to determine her own treatment and destiny.

She started the Gerson Therapy on November 15, 1995 at the Gerson Hospital and stayed there till December 5th, then returned home where she religiously followed the full program for two years. After that she switched to a modified program of three to four juices daily and a coffee enema every other day.

After seven months on the full Therapy finances became a problem. Barbara returned to full-time work as a psychiatric social worker at the Veterans Administration Hospital, but had to hire a helper to make juices to take to work and make the enema coffee. She had to move closer to work in order to go home at lunch break for juices, a meal and an enema. This has proved workable but not easy, and expensive.

She had frequent follow-ups with the Gerson doctor. Her

n

co-workers, physicians, nurses and other staff at the Veterans Hospital where she worked all showed support and much curiosity about her progress. One local physician told her that she should have been dead in six months. Barbara replied, "I would have been if I had done chemo or radiation."

She adds, "I feel strongly that to follow the Gerson program religiously, a person must be determined and convinced that the program can cure cancer and that one must persevere in spite of all the obstacles. I am very sad that the American medical establishment is against non-chemical treatments that work, especially since what they have to recommend obviously fails."

Diagnosis made at the Bayfront Medical Center, St.Petersburg, Florida, on October 17 1995: Bilateral ovarian cancer.

Debbi Wagner — Ovarian Cancer

In January 1995, Debbi went to the San Antonio Community Hospital in Upland County for a routine vaginal hysterectomy with rectocele repair. During surgery they found multiple nodules on the upper vaginal cuff. A subsequent exploratory laparotomy disclosed cancer on the ovaries, bowel, omentum and pelvic gutter. A more extensive hysterectomy had to be carried out through the stomach, removing the ovaries and omentum, and scraping the bowel and pelvic gutter as much as possible. Three nodules on the small bowel and right pelvic gutter, measuring less than 1.0 cm in size, were left; so were seedlings on the vaginal wall.

Debbi's condition turned out to be Stage III papillary serous ovarian carcinoma with extensive omental involvement, studding of the bowel and right gutter, as well as involvement of both ovaries. The doctors wanted her to have chemotherapy (Taxol and Cisplatin). Debbi felt scared and visited the UCLA Medical Center for a second opinion. Contrary to her hopes, the original diagnosis was confirmed, so she arranged with a doctor near her home to start chemotherapy.

Her prognosis was not good: the experts said she probably had six to nine months to live. Upon this her father and uncle pushed her into considering the Gerson Therapy instead of chemotherapy.

Debbi read Dr. Gerson's book, *A Cancer Therapy: Results of 50 Cases,* watched the Gerson videos, did some research into chemotherapy and some other treatments. She asked UCLA and her oncologist for names of patients who were alive five years after undergoing chemotherapy for ovarian cancer. They didn't give her any. However, the Gerson Institute and the Cancer Control Society in Los Angeles supplied her with patients' names and phone numbers. She 'phoned these individuals, who had all had the same stage of ovarian cancer as she had, or even higher. They were alive 9, 10, 14 and 17 years after their original diagnosis with no recurrences, having used the Gerson Therapy — and feeling great.

The Gerson Therapy really made sense. Debbi canceled her chemo the day before she was to start it and decided to go to Mexico to start the Gerson Therapy. Her family and friends fully supported her decision.

Two years after that nightmarish diagnosis, Debbi had no sign of any recurrence, and all her tests showed clear. Way back in February 1995, two weeks after her original surgery, an MRI found a cyst on her left kidney, and gallstones. All that has vanished. Her adult onset diabetes is also controlled. She does not have to take any hormones to control the body changes due to the removal of her ovaries, and is free from the panic attacks that used to trouble her since childhood.

Debbi recalls three women acquaintances of hers who had ovarian cancer and were treated with chemotherapy. None of them lived even for nine months. She is the only survivor. She is deeply grateful to Dr Gerson and to her own family and friends for having helped her through her ordeal and adds, "I am much healthier and more active than I have ever been." Debbi appeared in The Gerson Miracle in 2004.

Diagnosis from the San Antonio Community Hospital, Upland, CA, January 26 1995:

Well-differentiated papillary carcinoma with extension to serosal surface of left ovary. Metastatic papillary adenocarcinoma of uterus. Metastatic papillary adenocarcinoma of right ovary.

Aurora Lamb — Ovarian Cancer

In 1978, in Hilo, Hawaii, during one of her regular check- ups, Aurora at age 29 had a Pap smear. Her doctor asked her if she had any problems. She said that she was sore on one side. The doctor further examined her and told her that it was probably a cyst. He scheduled surgery to remove it.

In the course of the operation, the surgeon found a mass extending to both ovaries. He did a total hysterectomy, of course removing both ovaries. At that time, tissue was also turned over for a biopsy.

When Aurora woke up, the doctor told her that she had ovarian cancer, Stage III. Even the doctor was shocked to find such an advanced disease at that early age. He did suggest the usual treatments: chemotherapy and radiation. Meantime, a friend of Aurora's who had read the book by Jaquie Davison, Cancer Winner, lent it to Aurora. Jaquie's book tells the story of her recovery from widespread, terminal melanoma by the Gerson Therapy. Aurora then obtained Dr. Gerson's *A Cancer Therapy: Results of 50 Cases,* and was further interested. She and her husband decided at that point to visit the Cancer Control Society's convention, which took place over the Fourth of July weekend in Los Angeles. During the convention, they heard many speakers but found that the Gerson Therapy made the most sense. Aurora and her husband were really impressed and she then spent one week at the Mexican Gerson hospital to learn the details of the Therapy.

While Aurora's husband and her own family were supporting her decision, there was some fairly heavy opposition from her husband's brother, an MD. It is interesting that, eventually, her brother-in-law was swayed in the direction of the Gerson Therapy, and even used some of its principles for himself.

Meantime, Aurora did the Gerson Therapy strictly for two years, then continued with a less strict approach, "on and off," as she said. In time they adopted a daughter who is now (Feb. '02) 16 years old. Aurora runs her own business, also does crafts, travels and enjoys life. She still does enemas occasionally and drinks some juices, and remains "very well." She feels that the right mindset is most important. She will also be glad to talk to other prospective patients.

Madelyn Handlong — Uterine Cancer

Madelyn was 62 years old when in the course of a regular annual checkup and Pap smear the doctor noted that she was bleeding from the uterus. Madelyn thought that, surprisingly, she was still having a period. But the doctor performed a D & C and discovered that, in fact, Madelyn was suffering from uterine cancer — malignant cells were found in the scraped tissue.

That surprised her, too, since she had been careful to eat "healthfully" since 1957. At that time she was suffering from bursitis. The movements of her shoulder were so restricted that she was unable to comb her hair or swim. She read an article in *Prevention,* which suggested Brewers' Yeast as a remedy for bursitis. Madelyn tried it and found that after about three weeks of taking some tablespoonfuls of Brewers' Yeast her sleep had improved and her arm was moving much better. She had also changed her diet.

With the diagnosis of a malignancy in the uterus, her doctors wanted to do a hysterectomy, followed by radiation. Madelyn spent a few days at the hospital, but, in her own words, she "couldn't stand it." She refused the suggested treatments. Her husband had a copy of Dr. Gerson's book, *A Cancer Therapy,* which he had bought second-hand and had also lent it out. Madelyn decided to give the Gerson Therapy a try, and in 1985 went to the Gerson Hospital in Mexico for a month.

Meantime her daughter helped her to get the Gerson Therapy household established at home – she even found a second-hand Norwalk juicer — while Madelyn "just loved the Therapy, it was my kind of thing." Her uterine bleeding had stopped after the D & C.

Madelyn's condition improved greatly and after about six months she went down from 13 juices to about seven a day. She continues to be very well, now in her mid-seventies, is active and working hard in her family's plant nursery business.

Lynn von Schneidau — Endometriosis

At the age of 22, Lynn developed endometriosis, a disease that causes bleeding tumors in various parts of the body. In her case the tumors settled in her left ovary and on her sciatic nerve, causing her excruciating pain for several days every month. For a year she tried to deal with the pain unaided, then began seeing doctors and was diagnosed with endometriosis.

The first doctors she visited said they could prescribe Danocrine, or else Lynn could get pregnant, which was not an option for her at the time. The alternative, Danocrine, turned out to be a male hormone which would make the patient gain weight, grow facial hair and develop a deeper voice. What Lynn was not told was that the drug could also damage her liver and kidneys and make her brain swell. She only took the drug for a short time – the ill effects made her stop fast. Eight other drugs were prescribed, but her pain was getting worse. A diagnostic laparoscopy, to confirm the diagnosis of endometriosis and allow the surgeon to cauterize any visible tumors, was also followed by worsening pain.

Eventually Lynn discontinued all drugs and went as an in-patient to Scripps Hospital in La Jolla, CA. There the doctors prescribed psychiatric treatment and a second "diagnostic" surgery, during which they would cauterize any obvious tumors, remove Lynn's appendix (because they felt it had no purpose), cut the nerves in her back to ease the pain on her sciatic nerve, and, with or without her consent, perform a full hysterectomy.

Hearing about this plan, Lynn decided to try instead the Gerson Therapy, which her mother knew about, and shortly afterwards, in March 1986, arrived at the Gerson Hospital in Mexico. Within two weeks on the full therapy, she had no more endometrial pain. She stayed on the intensive therapy for three months with the help of her family, then followed the modified version for one year. Three years later she got married and had three healthy babies in five years. She remains healthy, continues to eat organic foods and drinks three juices per day.

Busy though she is with three small children, Lynn has started studying at the John Bastyr University in Seattle, WA, to become a naturopathic physician. This is what she has to stay about her life-saving experience:

"My life completely changed as a result of the Gerson Therapy. My views of eating healthfully and taking responsibility for one's own health are the result of Gerson's philosophy. I hope to be able to give other people what I was given."

Echo Maillet — Cervical Cancer, Degenerative Malignant Bone Disease

My family history: baby brother died of a blood clot, nineteen year old brother died of a malignant brain tumor, father died at the age of 50 of bone cancer, mother died at 51 years (after radiation treatments for cancer of the uterus) of sclerosis of the liver from alcoholism, two uncles had bowel cancer, and on the list goes. Growing up having spent more time visiting loved ones in a hospital than seeing them at home was not my idea of a good childhood.

Due to our upbringing I grew up looking like the Michelin Tire man and struggled with my weight for years, and I also had extremely difficult menstrual cycles. In my early 20s I was diagnosed with anal fistulas, hemorrhoids, bleeding bowels, and diverticulitis. At that time doctors wanted to remove part of my bowels. I decided to take a look at my lifestyle and made some dietary changes. Since my family history of illness was strongly imprinted on my heart, I did not want to be another statistic — there had to be a better way! After attending some seminars, reading and researching some alternative therapies, I became a Lacto-Ovo-Vegetarian. This change certainly had an impact on my health, however it did not offer me a cure. I functioned for several years after that still having some bowel discomforts, difficult menstrual cycles and was still overweight.

In my mid-thirties, after my son was born, I was diagnosed with cervical cancer (stage 4). I was scheduled for surgery 10 days after I was diagnosed. I promptly went home and discontinued all animal products (milk, cheese, eggs) and went on a very clean diet of only fresh fruit, vegetables and a small amount of cooked grains for the next 10 days. On the pre-op tests my stage of cancer had dropped from 4 to 1. It was then evident to me more than ever how our lifestyle and eating habits directly affect our health. I canceled the surgery and continued my research into alternative health. We became Vegan, although we still ate a lot of cooked foods, meat analogs, seasonings, salt and oils. But we were careful not to eat any animal products!

Even with my new healthy lifestyle, my health continued to fail. I started to have extreme back problems. My son was delivered via a Cesarean section with long labor and a uterine infection. It was a difficult delivery done under spinal freezing that had been attempted four times by an internist that missed. This left a lot of damage and scar tissue in that area. So as the pain increased to the point where I was not able to function in the daily home duties and physical therapists, chiropractors and medical specialists could not relieve it, I was diagnosed with Degenerative Bone Disease. It had appeared that the cancer had spread from the cervix to the weakened spine.

At this point I had little function of my arms, they were very weak and I was in constant pain all over with shooting pains to the lower spine causing me to literally fall to the floor. There were three large abdominal tumors (it was never determined if they were benign or malignant), which had distended my abdomen enough to make people ask if I was pregnant. I was resistant to take further tests outside of X-rays, blood work or physical examination. I did not want to travel down the well-worn path of orthodox medicine that had very little hope to offer in my hour of need.

So, back to the books I went. It was at this time that I started to apply the Gerson Therapy. I was familiar with the book by Dr. Max Gerson, *A Cancer Therapy: Results of 50 Cases,* and had read and shared it with others years before, however I did not take it seriously at that time for application in my own life, until now. I did not have access to the Gerson Primer, so I gleaned what I could from the book. It was difficult for me to obtain the Lugol's solution, thyroid pills, etc., therefore I went on a totally raw diet, eating only live, fresh organic food. I juiced on a regular basis and took coffee enemas. Within two weeks the constant pain had gone, though I still had some shooting pains, but they were subsiding. This already made my life more pleasant. Unfortunately that gave me fits of heroics and I would also do some physical tasks beyond my state of health. This soon made me see my place and restrain myself until the body could truly heal. Realizing that bones take up to a year to heal I took it quite easy, using the *Gerson Healing Newsletter* 15(1), 2000, a rebounder for gentle exercise, hot and cold hydrotherapy to assist the elimination of toxins in my system and to aid the healing. Along with the intense nutritional program and the detoxifying, I had a loving supportive family to guide and encourage me, this only added to round the whole thing off — how could I not get well?

So here I am over two years later — cancer free and all of my previous medical problems gone: arthritis, PMS, obesity, liver spots, tumors, migraines, depression, allergies, cancer, degenerative bone disease, chronic pain, even the "C-Section" scar — all gone! Remember that I had *no surgery, drugs or medical interventions!* Health or lack of it is generally our own doing. My condition was in obvious need of some intervention, however what was not so obvious was that my family was also in need of help. They never showed the severity of symptoms that I had, but rather often had the flu, colds, headaches and general fatigue and so-called yearly health problems that are considered to be "normal" today. We have since found out the truth. We have not had a cold, flu or so much as a sniffle in this home for years, even though we are exposed to people all the time as we conduct seminars, etc.

This has been a blessing for all members of the family — there are no more health problems for any of us.

Elizabeth Littlefield — Cervical and Uterine Cancer

Born in 1921, Elizabeth has a complex medical history. In 1967, aged 38, she was diagnosed with Stage 4 cancer of the cervix at Yale – New Haven (CT) Hospital. The cancer had already invaded the bladder wall. Prior to surgery she received 4500 rads of cobalt radiation, which shrank the tumor by 70%. During the long and complicated operation her uterus was found to be cancerous, too, and was removed, together with both ovaries, cervix and urinary bladder. Elizabeth withstood the surgery well and was able to return to work.

In the early Seventies she found out about the Gerson Therapy, and in 1977 went for a week to recently-opened Gerson Hospital in Mexico. She stayed on the Therapy for 18 months and experienced a significant improvement in her general health, together with a sense of rejuvenation. She remained on the modified Gerson Therapy "on and off" ever since, and returned for ten days to the Mexican Gerson Hospital for a "refresher" in 1987.

Her next serious problem arose in 1988, when she needed surgery for a fistula in the lower bowel, caused by the extensive radiation she had received in 1967. This was carried out at the White Memorial Hospital in Los Angeles, by Dr. Zerne. However, the radiation had also damaged the lymph nodes in Elizabeth's left groin, causing severe edema in her left leg. She has been able to control it to some extent, but it has not gone away completely.

In 1995, Elizabeth had a thorough check-up at Saddleback Radiology, Laguna Hills, CA, and was found to be free of metastatic malignant disease, being generally in good health. Now aged over 80, in a recent letter to Charlotte Gerson she wrote, "I know I will pass away one of these days, but I'll be d - - d if I die of cancer!"

Sonya Travis — Endometriosis, Cervical Cancer

Already as a young woman Sonya suffered from female problems; her menstruation was always difficult, with heavy bleeding that often contained large clots.

In due course she was diagnosed with endometriosis and had a number of D & C's (scraping of the uterus) to remove endometrial plaque. Finally, over 35 years ago, she underwent an operation in which the surgeon removed one ovary and part of the other.

Despite this intervention, her extremely heavy and painful periods with large blood clots persisted. A Pap smear in 1979 showed cancer of the cervix; she was also found to have "atypical" cells in her blood. At that point she was scheduled to have a total hysterectomy. She also had "lumps" in her breast and under her arm, but these were not further investigated or biopsied. But in view of the "atypical" cells in her blood, these may well have been malignant.

Sonya declined the hysterectomy — she "did not want to follow that route." Instead, she investigated some alternative methods and started by changing her diet and fasting. Many years earlier she had heard a talk given by Charlotte Gerson. At that time she decided that if anybody in her family ever had cancer, she would do the Gerson Therapy. So she went to the Gerson Hospital (at that time La Gloria) in Mexico.

In the course of her Gerson treatment Sonya was surprised when she experienced some severe healing reactions in her stomach area, with eating difficulties, nausea and vomiting. Then she remembered that some time before an iridologist (an expert studying the iris for signs of good or ill health) had told her that she had a good deal of scar tissue in her stomach and duodenum, possibly caused by earlier ulcers.

Sonya stayed on the Therapy for two years. She stresses that "never once did a bite of food enter my mouth that I should not have eaten."

Unfortunately Sonya's records were destroyed in a fire that severely damaged a section of the Mexican Hospital. Nevertheless, she remembers vividly the essentials of her long-term recovery from life-threatening disease on the Gerson Therapy.

She has remained in good shape, has great energy, and leads an extremely busy life, looking after her aged parents, her in-laws and grandchildren.

Elisabeth Curry — Cervical Cancer

Elisabeth was born in March 1953. Aged 29, in 1982, she was in the last year of studying to qualify as a chiropractor when she visited her mother at Christmas; it was there that she woke up one morning in pain and bleeding, and suddenly had the thought flashing through her mind: "I have cancer."

Her intuitive sensing turned out to be correct. The result of a Pap smear showed 'Class 5,' the designation for malignancy at the time. Further medical tests in Los Angeles included a colposcopy (a vaginal examination of cervical tissues to pinpoint areas for a biopsy), and Elisabeth underwent a cone biopsy on February 24, 1983. The report stated "Stage 1 A," malignant. This implied that the cancer had not invaded surrounding tissues, lymph nodes or blood vessels. Even so, her doctor said that a total hysterectomy had to be carried out, along with the removal of lymph nodes; however, he thought he could possibly save her ovaries.

Elisabeth refused the operation, since she was still hoping to have children; upon this her doctor predicted that she would be dead in two years' time.

Meanwhile, for the past year and a half she had also been suffering from debilitating migraines, which kept occurring more and more frequently. On top of it all she was also plagued with severe fatigue.

Despite all this, she wanted to complete her last term of chiro-practic training, but she also realized that her illness had to be dealt with. Having refused what orthodox medicine had to offer, she gathered information on various alternative systems of cancer treatment and health care, and found that the approach of the Gerson Therapy appealed to her most. Accordingly, in March 1983 she arrived at the Gerson hospital in Mexico, and although she only stayed for six days, she moved on for several months to the "Gerson Halfway House" in San Diego, where the correct food and fresh juices were available for Gerson patients. She had no other treatment of any kind.

Then she became pregnant. Her obstetrician suggested a termination, but he decided to re-examine her at the four months' point, to reconsider the options. To his surprise he found a lesion that looked more like scar tissue, and he saw no reason why Elisabeth should not complete her pregnancy. Her son was born exactly one year to the date when she was told about her biopsy result.

As a happy side effect of the Gerson Therapy, after embarking on it Elisabeth never suffered another migraine. She gave birth to a second baby, and also trained as a nurse practitioner, a profession in which she is now active, being very busy – and very well.

Last contact: March 2002. Elisabeth tells us, "Both my pregnancies went well, and the kids are now 18 and 15, bright and healthy. Neither has ever required antibiotics (nor have they had vaccines). I've had a couple of dozen Pap smears since 1983, and they've all been perfect."

Kidney Cancer

Josefine Petith — Kidney Cancer

In 1983, while traveling, Josefine aged 51, was unable to urinate. She was taken to the emergency clinic in Konstanz where her urine was drained. The attending physician did an X-ray as well as an ultra-sound. These tests showed a tumor on her left kidney, blocking her urethra. Immediate surgery was suggested.

Josefine had the operation at the Universitaets Klinik in Frankfurt, Germany, in August 1983. The biopsy showed the kidney malignancy and her left kidney was removed. Following the surgery, she suffered from severe weakness. She reports that she was unable to hold a cup of coffee in her hand. Her recovery was slow but complete.

Twelve years later, in 1995, while at her winter residence in Stuart, Florida, Josefine suffered from abdominal pain. On examination, the doctors found a tumor blocking her bile duct causing her to be jaundiced. On further check, it was discovered that she had 16 tumors throughout her abdomen and liver. Her doctor gave a desperate prognosis, told her husband that she had at most 6 months to live. The surgeon tried to remove some tumors but these were so extensive that removal was impossible. All he could do was to install a by-pass so that her bile could drain thus also relieving her of the jaundice.

For several years before this occurrence, Josefine as well as her husband were not only vegetarians, but ate mainly raw food.

When they received the desperate prognosis, they decided to try the Gerson Therapy and arrived at the Mexican Gerson Clinic during the winter of 1995. She was bedfast when she arrived, but started to feel better after a little more than a week. After she left the hospital, she continued the strict Gerson Therapy at home. Two years later, the same doctor who had told her that she had at most 6 months of life, re-examined her. He was truly happy, hugged her and congratulated her for her regained health. Even her liver was healed.

Josefine and her husband continued to eat mostly vegetarian foods. However, the propaganda of the supposed benefits of soy caused them to include considerable amounts of soy in their diet. Aside from that, Josefine also took some pastries, meat, and other foods not on the Gerson Therapy. She remained in good health for some 4 years. Then, in November of 2001, while vacationing on Tenerife, she noticed that 'her skirt was getting very tight.' She didn't believe that she could have gained weight so rapidly, and, on her return home to Germany, had a medical examination. The doctor in Bad Homburg discovered that she had many new tumors in her abdomen, a pancreas malignancy, as well as a 'large' mass in her liver and an enlarged 'tumorous' right kidney (her remaining one). In January 2002, she came back to Mexico for a return to the Gerson Therapy. Her latest report is that she is getting better again.

Sister Mary Moranda — Left Kidney Sarcoma
Case No. 38 in *A Cancer Therapy*

ister Moranda was born in 1903. In February 1945, she was operated on at the Sacred Heart Hospital, Allentown, PA, where a very large tumor weighing 23 lbs. was removed from her abdomen, with her kidney enclosed. The biopsy revealed that the category of the huge tumor was "a small, round and spindle cell kidney sarcoma." The surgeon felt that a recurrence was likely and decided that the patient should be given deep X-ray therapy.

Sister Moranda received 18 deep X-ray treatments in July and August 1946, then again 42 treatments the following year between June and August 1947. The side effects included vomiting, dizziness, secondary anemia, weakness and weight loss. She suffered from severe stomach upsets and bad constipation. Eventually she decided that she could no longer tolerate the hospital treatments.

In October 1947, when she first arrived at Dr. Gerson's office, she had a distended abdomen, a badly swollen left leg which she could hardly move or bend, and a large tumor mass in her left lower abdomen, just below the old operation scar. During the first two months of the treatment she was very weak and tired, but started to improve in the next three weeks. From then on she improved steadily. After one year on the Gerson Therapy, by September 1948, she was much stronger and no tumor could be felt. Also, her leg was back to normal size and motility. But, as Dr. Gerson noted, "It took her more than 1-1/2 years to recover from fear and anxiety."

In June 1954 she reported that she had been checked by doctors in Wedron, IL, and had been found free of cancer.

Sister Moranda lived to age 85, was well and active, teaching at the convent where she resided. In 1988, we received news of her death.

Healing the Gerson Way: Defeating Cancer and Other Chronic Diseases   by Charlotte Gerson and Beata Bishop

The best, most readable and useful Gerson Therapy book there is. Gerson and Bishop explain the rationale, science and method behind the Gerson Therapy, including 90 pages of recipes, guides to medication, case histories for cancer and many chronic illnesses. A must-have.   **$29.95**

Healing Arthritis the Gerson Way

Healing Arthritis is a complete how-to guide to for repairing and reversing arthritic conditions using the well-known Gerson Therapy. Charlotte Gerson includes the latest medical research on arthritis and the most common forms of the disease. Case histories of patients who have healed themselves of various arthritis, bone and joint diseases will inspire and motivate you. Easy to follow, instructions guide readers through the program ...

• How the Gerson Therapy helps to rebuild the immune system so that it stops and prevents arthritic conditions
• What equipment and foods are necessary for the Gerson Therapy
• Recipes and cooking techniques for preparing healthy foods and juices
• How to perform natural detoxification
• What patients can expect when doing the Therapy   **$19.95**

Lose Weight the Gerson Way

Lose weight easily, naturally and permanently using the proven and internationally known Gerson Therapy. In today's technologically advanced "better living though chemistry" world, you are constantly absorbing hazardous chemicals from the air, water, food and environment. Combining this toxic load with a diet of nutritionally deficient, genetically modified, pesticide laden, pre-packaged foods high in sugar, salt, fat, preservatives, artificial flavors, dyes, and sweeteners, you are being programmed to give in to cravings and eat more food than you need. The standard scientific model of too many calories taken in and too few calories burned off is not the only factor in weight gain. In fact, recent research shows the chemicals and toxins you absorb interfere with the body's metabolism to favor retention, no matter how much you diet and exercise. Fortunately, now that you know the cause of the problem, you can solve it using the Gerson Therapy, an all-natural, nutrition building and detoxification program that will empower you to lose weight and keep it off for good!   **$19.95**

Healing Diabetes the Gerson Way

Healing Diabetes the Gerson Way provides a powerful program to reverse type 2 diabetes and return you to complete health. Healing Diabetes is an easy-to-follow, how-to guide for using the Gerson Therapy to overcome type 2 diabetes. The simple step-by-step instructions cover everything you need to know and guide you through each part of the program.

Here is some of what's included ...

• The latest in scientific research on the causes of type 2 diabetes
• Foods and equipment necessary to implement the Gerson Therapy
• 90 pages of Gerson-approved recipes for healthy foods and juices
• Complete instructions for performing the natural detoxification process
• Hints and tips to make the Therapy easier   **$19.95**

Healing High Blood Pressure the Gerson Way

Based on the work of Dr. Max Gerson, the Gerson Therapy for high blood pressure will help you to open clogged arteries, lower elevated blood pressure, lose weight, reduce stress and return to complete health. It is commonly known that poor dietary and lifestyle choices lead to increased blood pressure. It also known high blood pressure can be eliminated by making the right choices and that is what this program is all about. Gerson Therapy is an all-natural method of reversing high blood pressure that eliminates its causes and restores your body's natural defenses so it will repair damage already done. Easy to follow instructions guide you through every part of the program. Here is some of what's included ...

• How the Gerson Therapy works to rebuild the immune system
• What foods and equipment are necessary for the Gerson Therapy
• Techniques and recipes for preparing healthy foods and juices
• Complete instructions for performing the natural detoxification process
• What to expect when doing The Therapy   **$19.95**

Gerson Movies

The Beautiful Truth

Follow Garrett on a cross-country trip to investigate the Gerson Therapy. He meets with cancer survivors who tell stories of triumph and healing by following the Gerson Therapy. Garrett interviews scientists, doctors and researchers, who reveal it is in the best interest of the medical industry to dismiss the notion of alternative and natural cures.   **$19.95**

26

Dying To Have Known

Filmmaker Steve Kroschel presents patients, scientists, surgeons and nutritionists who discuss the Gerson Therapy's efficacy in reversing cancer and degenerative diseases and show scientific proof to back up their claims. Interviews include a Japanese medical professor who cured himself of liver cancer, a lymphoma patient diagnosed as terminal over 50 years ago, and more. **$19.95**

The Gerson Miracle

This film introduces Dr. Max Gerson who developed a remedy for cancer and most chronic diseases over 80 years ago. The Gerson Therapy employs a diet and detoxification regimen to rebuild the immune system and restore the body's ability to heal itself. Former patients talk about their recoveries and Dr. Gerson's daughter, Charlotte discusses the medical and pharmaceutical industries and why they fear an all-natural therapy that allows people to take control of their own health. **$19.95**

The Gerson Movie Collection on Blu-ray

All three Gerson movies on one Blu-ray disc.
- The Beautiful Truth
- Dying to Have Known
- The Gerson Miracle **$24.95**

Books and DVDs available from:

Gerson Health Media
316 Mid Valley Center #230, Carmel, CA 93923
(831) 625-3565
info@gersonmedia.com | www.gersonmedia.com

The Gerson Institute
P.O. Box 161358, San Diego, CA 92176
(619) 685-5353 | Fax: (619) 685-5363
Toll Free in US (888) 4-GERSON (4437766)
info@gerson.org | www.gerson.org

Permission to use the Gerson® and Gerson Therapy® marks has been granted by The Gerson Institute. Contact the Gerson Institute to find out more about merchandise, services and educational programs concerning the Gerson Therapy.

CPSIA information can be obtained
at www.ICGtesting.com
Printed in the USA
LVHW022112030423
743361LV00034B/1611

9 781937 920074

The
Scuppernong Press
Wake Forest, NC

Miss Belle Boyd

By
Richard Lee Montgomery

Living in the Land of Cotton Biography Series
Miss Belle Boyd

©2017 Richard Lee Montgomery

First Printing

The Scuppernong Press
PO Box 1724
Wake Forest, NC 27588
www.scuppernongpress.com

Cover and book design by Frank B. Powell, III

International Standard Book Number ISBN 978-1-942806-13-4

Library of Congress Control Number: 2017954440

— Table of Contents —

— Introduction to Series —

As a member of the Sons of Confederate Veterans and for every other member, we have been charged to stand in *"the defense of the Confederate soldier's good name, the guardianship of his history, the emulation of his virtues, the perpetuation of those principles which he loved."* Through my website, the books I have published and the lectures I have given, are all about keeping the Confederate culture alive in this cynical time of America's history.[1]

For my life, I have committed it to living a lifestyle which would be pleasing to the Lord Jesus Christ. However, knowing that I can easily displease Him and therefore diminish His glory, there are foundational tools which have been a constant reminder for me in seeking to glorify my God. Seeking to live for the Lord Jesus Christ, I have learned to strive in developing a prayer life and equally allowing a healthy time in the reading of the Word of God, which can bring direction and focus.

My point is, this can easily describe many of the leaders of the Confederacy as well as those on the battlefield as soldiers. In fact, the Confederate Constitution teaches to us what was of most importance to them, *"We, the people of the Confederate States, each State acting in its sovereign and independent character, in order to form a permanent federal government, establish justice, insure domestic tranquility and secure the blessings of liberty to ourselves and our posterity — invoking the favor and guidance of Almighty God — do ordain and establish this Constitution for the Confederate States of America."*[2]

---

[1]livinginthelandofcotton.com
[2]Constitution of the Confederate States of America (Milledgeville: Georgia State Convention, 1861), 2.

I find the phrase *"invoking the favor and guidance of Almighty God,"* as a foundational statement in this new constitution. It teaches us there was a culture which was very important to the South before, during and after the years of 1861-1865. In this new series of biographies, the reader will see that there were men and women who fought for the protection of their families, homes, towns, cities, states and country by an invading army. The reader will see there were those who held to Christian principles and at the same time, fought for States' Rights and held this principle high.

I am not suggesting that this new government was a Christian (theocratic) nation because there were many who were not Christians, but who also fought for States' Rights. Also, there were many who did not know anything about this constitutional right issue — they just knew they did not want anyone dictating to them and their families what they can and cannot do.

This series is based on primary sources. By that I mean they are books published before "Lincoln's War" and books published going into the 1930s. Much of what you will read are quotes and narratives from these sources. At times, I will interject my thoughts but centered on what the source stated. The desired outcome for this new series is that the reader might be inspired, encouraged and become more proactive for the truths of history.

I hope you enjoy this biography,

Richard Lee Montgomery

Miss Belle Boyd

Born: May 9, 1844. in Martinsburg, Virginia.

Husbands: Samuel Wilde Hardinge (1864-1866), John Swainston Hammond (1869-1884), Nathaniel Rue High (1885-1900).

Children: Grace Hardinge, Marie Hammond, Byrd Hammond, John Hammond, Grace Hardinge, Arthur Hammond.

Death: June 11, 1900, Kilbourn City, Columbia County, Wisconsin (Today's name is Wisconsin Dells).

Buried: Spring Grove Cemetery, Wisconsin Dells, Wisconsin.

"On the evening of the 23rd May I was sitting at the window of our room, reading to my grandmother and cousin, when one of the servants rushed in, and shouted, or rather shrieked — 'Oh, Miss Belle, I t'inks de revels am a-comin', for de Yankees are a-makin' orful fuss in de street.' I immediately sprang from my seat and went to the door, and I then found that the servant's report was true. The streets were thronged with Yankee soldiers, hurrying about in every direction, in the greatest confusion." [3]

[3]Belle Boyd, *Belle Boyd: In Camp And Prison*, Volume 1 (London: Saunders, Otley & Company, 1865), 124-125.

W hen it comes to the *"War of Northern Ag-gression"* or *"Lincoln's War,"* there were those standout women from both the North, as well as from the South. **Maria Isabella "Belle" Boyd** was one of those women for the South or as we know it — the Confederate States of America.

Boyd

Miss Belle served the Confederacy as a Confederate spy and went to great extremes to deliver information to **General Stonewall Jackson.** Inter-

estingly, she began spying as a teenager at seventeen. Belle Boyd would report what she saw and heard from the Union soldiers who were stationed outside of her house. And then, she went to such extremes, as to walk and then run out onto battlefield in order to supply the Confederate Army with the information. Amazingly, from the start of the war, Belle realized what **Abraham Lincoln** was doing. She said, *"Politically I did not like Mr. Lincoln for*

Jackson

in him I saw the destroyer. As long as it served his purpose, Mr. Lincoln boldly advocated the right of Secession."[4] This teaches us that the topic of "secession" was not just an adult conversation.

Lincoln

But **Belle Boyd's** highest goal is stated in this manner, *"Hope, fear, the love of life, and the determination to serve my country to the last, conspired to fill my heart with more than feminine courage, and to lend preternatural strength and swiftness to my limbs. I often marvel and even shudder when I reflect how I cleared the fields and bounded over the*

---

[4]Belle Boyd, *Belle Boyd: In Camp and Prison, Volume 2* (London: Saunders, Otley & Company, 1865), 273.

Boyd

fences with the agility of a deer."[5] Simply stated, she only wanted to help her people and her country — the South.

---

[5]Belle Boyd, *Belle Boyd: In Camp and Prison, Volume 1* (London: Saunders, Otley & Company, 1865), 133.

— Miss Belle's Formative Years —

Miss Belle describes her beginnings as only she can, *"There is, perhaps, no tract of country in the world more lovely than the Valley of the Shenandoah. There is, or rather, I should say, there was, no prettier or more peaceful little village than Martinsburg, where I was born, in [May 9] 1844."*[6]

In his book, *Belle Boyd: Confederate Spy*, Louis A. Sigaud says, *"Born at Martinsburg on May 9, 1844, Belle was named Isabelle in honor of a great-aunt. Belle's godmother and her grandmother, Maria, were sisters who had married brothers: John and Samuel Boyd respectively. John and Isabella Boyd, after their marriage in 1803, had left Virginia and settled in Knoxville, Tennessee, but they kept in close touch with their Martinsburg kin, and were delighted when young Mary*[7] *and Benjamin*[8] *became parents.*

Though Belle was born in Martinsburg, probably at the home of her grandmother, Mrs. Samuel Boyd, she was soon taken to Bunker Hill, a crossroads hamlet some ten miles away. Here her parents had a pleasant two-storied house with walls completely hidden by roses and honeysuckle, the memory of which remained with Belle always. Around the house silver maples swayed their branches gently in breezes heavy with the scent of flowers in summer; and before it, at a short distance,

---

[6]Ibid., 34.
[7]Mary Rebecca Glenn
[8]Benjamin Reed Boyd

Mill Creek flowed swiftly a cheerfully talkative stream on an urgent, never-ending errand from the mountains to the sea." [9]

Washington City

"Sometime between 1849 and 1854 Benjamin Boyd, who had a general store at Bunker Hill, erected a stone building on Queen Street east of the railroad in Martinsburg, moved his store there and brought his family to live at 126 East Burke Street. At this time Benjamin was also directing a tobacco plantation. ... During her childhood Belle enjoyed the constant companionship of younger brothers and sisters,[10] and probably saw much of her numerous young cousins. Outside her family, her particular playmates were her neighbors, Virginia and Betty Doll." [11]

But the bottom line, as Miss Belle explains, *"I passed my childhood as all happy children usually do, petted and caressed by a father and mother, loving and beloved by my brothers and sisters."* [12]

Mount Washington Cottage

Also, *"according to the custom of my country, I was sent at twelve years of age to* **Mount Washington College**,[13] *of which Mr. Staley, of whom I cherish a most grateful recollection, was then principal. At sixteen my education was supposed to be completed, and I made my entree into the world in* **Washington City** *with all the high hopes and thoughtless joy natural to my time of life. I did not then dream how soon my youth was to be 'blasted with a curse' the worst that can befall man or woman — the curse of civil war."* [14]

---

[9]Louis A. Sigaud, *Belle Boyd: Confederate Spy* (Richmond: The Dietz Press, 1944), 2.
[10]William, Benjamin Jr., Anna, Mary and Annie.
[11]Ibid., 3.
[12]Belle Boyd, *Belle Boyd: In Camp and Prison, Volume 1* (London: Saunders, Otley & Company, 1865), 38.
[13]Located in Baltimore, Maryland.
[14]Ibid., 39.

— Lincoln's War of Aggression Has Arrived —

Miss Belle gives her opinion of **Abraham Lincoln**: *"Politically I did not like Mr. Lincoln, for in him I saw the destroyer. As long as it served his purpose, Mr. Lincoln boldly advocated the right of Secession. I trust that the accusation will not startle my readers; but such was the case; and I will cite one instance — when, as a representative, he openly avowed 'that any nation or people in any portion of the world had a right to rise up and rebel against the mother-government if they wanted to.'"* [15]

Boyd   Lincoln

Though so eager to enjoy the happiness due her budding womanhood, the clear-thinking young girl, fresh from school at Baltimore, understood what was happening. Conscious of no need to make a decision as to her own allegiance, she engaged in no soul-searching. As she saw it, Lincoln's election had made the secession of Southern States certain. The North really intended more than the freedom of the Negro. It also meant to exclude the landed proprietors of the South from participation m national legislation. This she thought was particularly true of the New England merchants. To such an arrogant attempt to dominate, harness, and enslave the South, to such a threat to change its pleasant, leisurely, manorial way of life to a frenzied tempo of incessant trading for profit, the intensely partisan Southern girl saw but one answer. There remained, she believed firmly, but one effective way to make it.

---

[15] Belle Boyd, *Belle Boyd: In Camp and Prison, Volume 2* (London: Saunders, Otley & Company, 1865), 273-274.

Virginia's Stars and Bars

South Carolina was first to secede. Other States followed her lead, and the cruel prospect of civil war became a far more dreadful reality. President Lincoln asked the States to furnish recruits for the service of the United States, and fixed a quota for each State. The Old Dominion supplied the men but, as Belle wrote proudly and still defiantly four years later, Virginia provided them for the Stars and Bars. Her own place was no longer in Washington. Without delay, she left the Capital for her Valley.

Jackson

In that magnificent land [16] of incomparable beauty and bounteous plenty, the forces of the North and of the South were destined to fight back and forth savagely and incessantly. On the floor of the Valley, in its gently-rolling hills, and on its high, rugged mountains, its own knightly **Ashby** was to lead the cavaliers of his famed Laurel Brigade to great deeds; the Stonewall Brigade was to march and fight its way to renown; and the military genius of **Jackson** [17] was to write its immortal saga with his mighty sword on the pages of history."[18]

Ashby

All in all, Miss Belle's position on secession was built on strong convictions. In fact, even when she was captured by the Yankees *"in the summer of 1862, Leslie's Weekly* [19] reported the glad tidings that, 'Belle Boyd, the Secesh Cleopatra, is caged at last'..."* [20] Miss Belle believed as most Southerners did, in the sovereignly of the states and their right of secession. It

---

[16]Before Virginia was divided into two separate states.
[17]Thomas Jonathan "Stonewall" Jackson
[18]Louis A. Sigaud, *Belle Boyd: Confederate Spy* (Richmond: The Dietz Press, 1944), 6-7.
[19]Leslie's Weekly Magazine
[20]Ibid., 100.

was this passion and devotion to the South and their cause, that led her to serve the Confederacy, regardless of what the consequences might be.

Washington City

Having just graduated from **Mount Washington College** in 1860, at which time she shortened her name to simply *"Belle."* After graduation, she moved to **Washington City** in the winter of 1860-1861. With the nation's turmoil brewing, Miss Belle returned to her family in Martinsburg, in time for her Virginia to secede from the Union. Many of the Boyd clan enlisted in the Confederate Army and for the cause for which it stood. Miss Belle's father Benjamin joined the Second Virginia Infantry Regiment, that would become part of the Stonewall Brigade.[21] We are told that he was *"forty-four, and not a man given to much physical activity, he decided someone else could run the store."* [22]

Mount Washington Cottage

For young *Miss Belle*, she would become an espionage agent — a spy, when she was just seventeen years old and served the Confederacy, in the North as well as in England.[23] However, before becoming a spy for the Confederacy, Miss Belle shot a Union soldier who

Boyd

was trying to raise a Union flag over her home. She describes this event in this manner, *"They had brought with them a large Federal flag, which they were now preparing to hoist over our roof in token of our submission to their authority; but to this my mother would not consent. Stepping forward with a firm step, she said, very quietly, but resolutely, 'Men, every member of my household will die before that flag shall be raised over us.'*

---

[21]Ibid., 8.
[22]Ibid., 8.
[23]Ibid., 147.

Upon this, one of the soldiers, thrusting himself forward, addressed my mother and myself in language as offensive as it is possible to conceive. I could stand it no longer; my indignation was roused beyond control; my blood was literally boiling in my veins; I drew out my pistol and shot him. He was carried away mortally wounded, and soon after expired.

… In the meantime it had been reported at head-quarters that I had shot a Yankee soldier, and great was the indignation at first felt and expressed against me. Soon, however, the commanding officer, with several of his staff, called at our house to investigate the affair. He examined the witnesses, and inquired into all the circumstances with strict impartiality, and finally said I had 'done perfectly right.' He immediately sent for a guard to headquarters, where the elite of the army was stationed and a tolerable state of discipline preserved.

Sentries were now placed around the house, and Federal officers called every day to inquire if we had any complaint to make of their behaviour. It was in this way that I became acquainted with so many of them; an acquaintance 'the rebel spy' did not fail to turn to account on more than one occasion." [24]

Jackson

Miss Belle put herself in dangerous situations: she galloped into the dark with ciphered messages and; she stealthily maneuvered herself into rooms, to eavesdrop, on Union Army conferences. On her most famous act of espionage for the Confederacy, occurred on May 23, 1862. After obtaining the status location of Union forces at Front Royal, Virginia, she ran on foot from town — through crossfire to meet the advancing Confederates. The information she brought was a confirmation of **General Jackson's** already information, permitting him to quickly capture the town.

---

[24]Belle Boyd, *Belle Boyd: In Camp and Prison, Volume 1* (London: Saunders, Otley & Company, 1865), 67-70.

According to her book *Belle Boyd: In Camp and Prison, Volume 1*, she tells the reader at length, *"The intelligence I was in possession of instructed me that **General Banks**[25] was at Strasbourg with four thousand men, that the small force at Winchester could be readily reinforced by* General White,[26] *who was at Harper's Ferry, and that Generals Shields and Geary were a short distance below Front Royal, while Fremont*[27] *was beyond the Valley; further, and this was the vital point, that it had been decided all these separate divisions should co-operate against **General Jackson**.*

Banks, White, Fremont & Jackson

I again went down to the door, and this time I observed, standing about in groups, several men who had always professed attachment to the cause of the South. I demanded if there was one among them who would venture to carry to General Jackson the information I possessed. They all with one accord said, 'No, no. You go.'

I did not stop to reflect. My heart, though beating fast, was not appalled. I put on a white sun-bonnet, and started at a run down the street, which was thronged with Federal officers and men. I soon cleared the town and gained the open fields, which I traversed with unabated speed, hoping to escape observation until such time as I could make good my way to the Confederate line, which was still rapidly advancing.

I had on a dark blue dress, with a little fancy white apron over it; and this contrast of colours, being visible at a great distance, made me far more conspicuous than was just then agreeable. The skirmishing between the outposts was sharp. The main forces of the opposing armies were disposed as follows: —The Federals had placed their artillery upon a lofty eminence, which commanded the road by which the Confederates were advancing.

---

[25]Nathaniel Prentice Banks
[26]Julius White
[27]John Charles Fremont, frontiersman with Kit Carson.

Their infantry occupied in force the hospital buildings, which were of great size, and sheltered by which they kept up an incessant fire.

The Confederates were in line directly in front of the hospital, into which their artillerymen were throwing shells with deadly precision; for the Yankees had taken this as a shelter, and were firing upon the Confederate troops from the windows. At this moment the Federal pickets, who were rapidly falling back, perceived me still running as fast as I was able, and immediately fired upon me.

My escape was most providential; for, although I was not hit, the rifle-balls flew thick and fast about me, and more than one struck the ground so near my feet as to throw the dust in my eyes. Nor was this all: the Federals in the hospital seeing in what direction the shots of their pickets were aimed, followed the example and also opened fire upon me.

Upon this occasion my life was spared by what seemed to me then, and seems still, little short of a miracle; for, besides the numerous bullets that whistled by my ears, several actually pierced different parts of my clothing, but not one reached my body. Besides all this, I was exposed to a cross fire from the Federal and Confederate artillery, whose shot and shell flew whistling and hissing over my head.

At length a Federal shell struck the ground within twenty yards of my feet; and the explosion, of course, sent the fragments flying in every direction around me! I had, however, just time to throw myself flat upon the ground before the deadly engine burst; and again Providence spared my life. Springing up when the danger was passed, I pursued my career, still under a heavy fire. I shall never run again as I ran on that, to me, memorable day. Hope, fear, the love of life, and the determination to serve my country to the last, conspired to fill my heart with more than feminine courage, and to lend preternatural strength and swiftness to my limbs. I often marvel and even shudder when I reflect how I cleared the fields and bounded over the fences with the agility of a deer.

As I neared our line I waved my bonnet to our soldiers, to intimate that they should press forward, upon which one regiment the 1st Maryland 'rebel' Infantry, and Hay's Louisiana Brigade, gave me a loud cheer, and, without waiting for further orders, dashed upon the town at a rapid pace.

They did not then know who I was, and they were naturally surprised to see a woman on the battle-field, and on a spot, too, where the fire was so hot. Their shouts of approbation and triumph rang in my ears for many a clay afterwards, and I still hear them not unfrequently in my dreams.

At this juncture the main body of the Confederates was hidden from my view by a slight elevation which intervened between me and them. My heart almost ceased to beat within me; for the dreadful thought arose in my mind that our force must be too weak to be any match for the Federals, and that the gallant men who had just been applauding me were rushing upon a certain and fruitless death. I accused myself of having urged them to their fate; and now, quite overcome by fatigue and by the feelings which tormented me, I sank upon my knees and offered a short but earnest prayer to God. Then I felt as if my supplication was answered, and that I was inspired with fresh spirits and a new life. Not only despair, but fear also forsook me; and I had again no thought but how to fulfil the mission I had already pursued so far.

I arose from my kneeling posture, and had proceeded but a short distance, when, to my unspeakable, indescribable joy, I caught sight of the main body fast approaching; and soon an old friend and connection of mine, Major Harry Douglas, rode up, and, recognizing me, cried out, while he seized my hand — 'Good God, Belle, you here! what is it?' 'Oh, Harry,' I gasped out, 'give me time to recover my breath.'

For some seconds I could say no more; but, as soon as I had sufficiently recovered myself, I produced the 'little note,' and told him all, urging him to hurry on the cavalry, with orders to them to seize the bridges before the retreating Federals should have time to destroy them.

He instantly galloped off to report to General Jackson, who immediately rode forward, and asked me if I would have an escort and a horse wherewith to return to the village. I thanked him, and said, 'No; I would go as I came;' and then, acting upon the information I had been spared to convey, the Confederates gained a most complete victory." [28]

Old Capitol Prison

Two months later, in July of 1862, Miss Bell was arrested by Union forces. In fact, it has been said that during a course of time, Miss Bell was placed under arrested six times, thrown in prison three times and exiled twice. But on this particular arrest, Miss Belle was sent to **Old Capitol Prison** in Washington, D.C. on July 29, 1862, the first time. *"WITHIN the famous prison, Belle was ushered into a small office. A clerk looked up casually and said her business would be attended to immediately. As he finished speaking, **Mr. Wood**,[29] the Superintendent, entered. A potent personage in official Washington, he was a powerfully built man of medium height, with brown hair, a fair complexion, and keen bluish-grey eyes.*

His greeting to her was: 'And so this is the celebrated rebel spy. I am very glad to see you, and will endeavor to make you as comfortable as possible. So whatever you wish for, ask for it and you shall have it. I am glad I have so distinguished a personage for my guest. Come, let me show you to your room.'

Wood

They crossed the hall, ascended a flight of stairs and came to a narrow passage with several doors opening upon it and a sentry pacing its length. Mr. Wood led her to Room No. 6 and informed her it was hers." [30]

---

[28]Ibid., 128-136.
[29]William Patrick Wood
[30]Louis A. Sigaud, *Belle Boyd: Confederate Spy* (Richmond: The Dietz Press, 1944), 76.

Ordered to interview **Miss Belle** were Superintendent **William Patrick Wood** and a **Mr. Lafayette Curry Baker**, chief of detectives of the War Department for the past six months had headed the National Detective Police. Miss Belle describes

Boyd, Wood & Baker

this interview: *"Belle's two callers were redoubtable enough to anticipate little difficulty in her case. They probably expected a routine performance ending with an admission of guilt and satisfactory expressions of repentance and abjuration.*

*Seating himself at her request, **Mr. Baker** promptly launched into an impressive but evidently habitual exhortation. He felt sure, he said, that she was already tired of prison life, mentioned casually that he had come to secure a confession regarding her offences against the Union cause, and suggested that, as the Federal authorities had plenty of proof, she might as well admit her guilt at once.*

Baker

'Sir,' she replied, with a knowledge of her rights, to be expected of a lawyer's niece, 'I do not understand you; and, furthermore, I have nothing to say. When you have informed me on what grounds I have been arrested, and given me a copy of the charges preferred against me, I will make my statement; but I shall not now commit myself.'

Unabashed by this first rebuff, Mr. Baker continued the usual procedure. He read aloud to her the oath of allegiance prisoners were customarily invited to take, waxed eloquent about the enormity of her offence, professed that the cause of the South was hopeless, and asked her to take the oath. Had she done so, she would, of course, have been released instantly. But then she would have been scorned and shunned by the South as a renegade, and forever distrusted by a Federal Government ready to charge her with treason if she ever again served the Confederacy.

Boyd

As Belle struggled to find words sufficiently vigorous and yet ladylike to answer him, Mr. Baker again pressed the oath upon her. Unwisely he reminded her that the dread Secretary of War, Mr. Stanton, who had sent him, would receive a faithful report of the interview. In a tone certain to be heard well beyond the door her inquisitors had carelessly left open, she retorted boldly: 'Tell Mr. Stanton from me, I hope that when I commence the oath of allegiance to the United States Government, my tongue may cleave to the roof of my mouth, and that if I ever sign one line that will show to the world that I owe the United States Government the slightest allegiance, I hope my arm may fall paralyzed by my side.'

Mr. Baker patiently recorded this outburst in a notebook, and then, realizing that he had failed to subdue this young rebel, declared angrily: 'Well, if this is your resolution, you'll have to lay here and die; and serve you right.'

Wood

But the thoroughly aroused Belle was now past all fear of restraint and punishment. Warming to her theme, and in a raised voice addressed more to the world at large than to her harassed tormentor, she cried out: 'If it is a crime to love the South, its cause, and its President, then I am a criminal. I am in your power; do with me as you please. But I fear you not, I would rather lie down in this prison and die, than leave it owing allegiance to such a government as yours. Now leave the room, for so thoroughly am I disgusted with your conduct towards me that I cannot endure your presence longer.

To her great surprise, she was answered by loud calls of 'Bravo! Bravo!' But these hearty explosions of approval were not uttered by the stunned Mr. Baker and Mr. Wood. They came from outside the open door, where delighted Confederate officers and English prisoners crowded about their own doors and hailed her outspoken denunciation of the Federal Government and its overtures with an enthusiastically responsive outburst.

At this point, **Superintendent Wood,** *who at the moment seemed to hold Mr. Baker in less esteem than usual, decided to intervene. Turning to his frustrated companion, he said curtly: 'Come, we had better go. The lady is tired.' And he prevailed upon him to leave."* [31]

On another occasion, **Miss Belle** was ar-rested in the summer of 1863, after return-ing to Martinsburg and finding out that it was now the Yankee state of West Virginia. She would be released in December and six months later, she volunteered to carry Confederate papers to England, aboard the blockade runner ***Greyhound***.

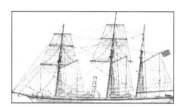

Greyhound

"In March I returned to Richmond, when, although somewhat recovered, my health still required care. I could not return home, and I felt, more-over, restless and unhappy at the death of my father. I determined, there-fore, to visit Europe so soon as I could arrange my affairs. When I made known this resolution to President Davis, he approved of the plan, consid-ering me to need quiet and rest in some place remote from the dangers of our sorely-pressed country.

Orders were given to the Confederate Secretary of State to make me the bearer of despatches. I commenced preparations for departing as speedily as possible.

The despatches were ready for me on March 25th, but a brief return of illness hindered me from starting, and, as these papers, being very impor-tant, could not be delayed, they were forwarded by some other hand.

---

[31]Ibid., 79-80.

Richmond

At last, on March 29th, I was able to leave **Richmond**, *having recovered sufficiently for travelling. Other despatches were now ready, and of them I was made the bearer.*

Owing to an accident on the railway, we did not arrive in Wilmington until several hours after the departure of the blockade-runner in which I was to have sailed.

This steamer would not be followed by another for at least a fortnight, because they did not run out during the brilliant nights of the full moon, lest they should fall an easy prey to Yankee blockaders. I was therefore obliged to await the arrival and departure of the next regular steamer, as, even putting aside all consideration of difficulties increased by moonlight, there was not a suitable craft in port.

One of the first vessels that arrived was the Greyhound, commanded by Captain 'Henry',[32] formerly, it is said, an officer in the United States navy,[33] and who had, at the commencement of the war, with many of his comrades, sent in his resignation to the United States Navy Department, and entered the Confederate service. Captain 'Henry' had formerly been on 'Stonewall' Jackson's staff; and, as I was acquainted with his family, I gladly accepted his kind invitation, and took passage on board the **Greyhound**, *feeling doubly secure under such a skillful commander."*[34]

Another passenger on board was **Edward Alfred Pollard**, an editor for the *Richmond Examiner*, said this of Captain Henry: "*What a splendid fellow he was: a graceful dash of manner, which yet beamed with intelligence, an exuberant hospitality, a kindness that when it did a*

---

[32]Known as king of blockade-runners, who was actually Lieutenant George Henry Bier.

[33]Ibid., 170.

[34]Belle Boyd, *Belle Boyd: In Camp and Prison, Volume 2* (London: Saunders, Otley & Company, 1865), 27-29.

grateful thing so gracefully waived all expressions of obligation, lie had been all over the world; was familiar with the great capitals of Europe; bore the marks of a wound obtained in the campaign of Stonewall Jackson; and as to his name and nationality — why, passengers on blockade-runners are not expected to be inquisitive of these circumstances, and must beware of impertinent curiosity." [35]

Pollard

In May 1864, according to the book *The War of the Sixties,* we are told, *"When the **Greyhound** was captured* [36] *— vessel and cargo adjudged by the Prize Court to be worth about half a million of dollars — among the passengers on board was the noted Belle Boyd, who had been a prisoner before, in the war, in the hands of General Butler, between whom and herself there had been a considerable amount of 'unpleasantness,' which had made her somewhat famous by her general conduct, with her speeches and pertness.*

*The **Greyhound** was taken to Boston, and, after having been adjudged lawful prize and condemned, Belle Boyd and the other passengers, the officers and crew, were all released and permitted to go where they pleased. From Boston they went to Halifax, and thence to England.*

Connecticut

---

[35]Edward A. Pollard, *Southern History of the War: The Third Year of the War* (New York: Charles B. Richardson, 1863), 324.
[36]The *Greyhound* was captured by the U.S.S. *Connecticut,* a Side-wheel Steamer.

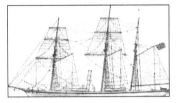

Greyhound

The prize-master of the **Greyhound** was a young volunteer officer [37] with the rank of acting-master in the United States Navy — rather a good-looking fellow. It seems that while on board of the **Greyhound** together, he and Belle Boyd became greatly interested in each other, which interest ripened into friendship. After they separated at Boston, a fervent correspondence sprung up and was continued between them, and they became engaged. She fascinated the prize-master to that degree that he turned traitor. He resigned from the Federal Navy, proceeded to England, and they were married in Liverpool, he, from that time, espousing the cause of, and fighting for, the South." [38]

Hardinge

---

[37]Sam Wilde Hardinge
[38]E. R. Hutchins, *The War of the Sixties* (New York: The Beale Publishing Company, 1912), 74-75.

— After Lincoln's War —

The couple had *one daughter, Grace,*[39] likely born in England before Sam Hardinge died in England between the end of 1865 and July 1866. Miss Belle married for a second time in 1869, to John Swainston Hammond. They had four children: Arthur who died in his first or second year;[40] Byrd Swainston, Marie Isabelle, and John Edmund.[41] The family moved from city to city, before settling in **Dallas** in 1883.

Dallas, Texas

Then *"On November 1st, 1884, the United States District Court in Dallas, Texas entered a decree granting Mrs. John S. Hammond (born Boyd) a divorce from her husband on the ground of cruel treatment, and awarded custody of the children to the mother."*[42] They were married just short of sixteen years.[43] Miss Belle married a third husband. This time to a Nathaniel Rue High on January 5, 1885.[44] Miss Belle was forty-one years old, while Nathaniel was only twenty-four years old, working for a stock company as an actor when they married.

---

[39]Louis A. Sigaud, *Belle Boyd: Confederate Spy* (Richmond: The Dietz Press, 1944), 186.
[40]Ibid., 192.
[41]Ibid., 192.
[42]Ibid., 193.
[43]Ibid., 193.
[44]Ibid., 195.

However, because of financial difficulties in the following year, Miss Belle took steps to provide for the family. *"On February 22, 1886, at the People's Theatre in Toledo, Belle Boyd presented for the first time a*

dramatic narrative of her activities as a Confederate agent. In an attractive **uniform of Confederate gray**, *wearing a broad, low-crowned hat with a large, flowing black plume reminiscent of General 'Jeb' Stuart, she came out before a stage background of battle and strife. After the moment of dramatic silence created by her impressive entrance, she fanned into immediate emotional response the memories of veterans who for twenty years had been reminiscing the war."* [45]

Belle in uniform

This became Miss Belle's method for supporting her family. She died of a heart attack on June 11, 1900, in **Kilbourn City**, Columbia County, Wisconsin (today Wisconsin Dells — which changed in 1931). She was lecturing on her career as a spy — before an audience of members of the Grand Army of the Republic — a Union Veterans' Association. She was touring the Western United States. Miss Belle is buried in **Spring Grove Cemetery**, Wisconsin Dells, Wisconsin.

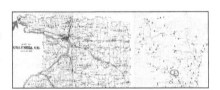

Then: Kildourn City,
Today: Wisconsin Dells

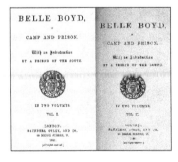

Miss Belle wrote a book entitled *Belle Boyd: In Camp and Prison*, while she lived in London in 1865 and has been republished many times. Her childhood house is located at 126 East Race Street in **Martinsburg, Virginia**, and her cottage is in **Front Royal, Virginia**, of which today they are museums.

---

[45]Ibid., 195-196.

To a close, I quote again from Louis Adrien Sigaud's book *Belle Boyd: Confederate Spy*, "*since her death hundreds of dramatic and controversial articles have been writ-*

Martinsburg, Virginia

Front Royal, Virginia

ten about the remarkable career of the woman known to so many as 'The Rebel Spy' and 'The Siren of the Shenandoah.' So she still lives on stirringly in the hearts of men and women fascinated and intrigued by these fragmentary recitals of her deeds." [46]

---

[46]Ibid., viii.

— Bibliography —

Constitution of the Confederate States of America (Milledgeville: Georgia State Convention, 1861).

Boyd, Belle, *Belle Boyd: In Camp And Prison*, Volume 1 (London: Saunders, Otley & Company, 1865).

Boyd, Belle, *Belle Boyd: In Camp and Prison*, Volume 2 (London: Saunders, Otley & Company, 1865).

Sigaud, Louis A., *Belle Boyd: Confederate Spy* (Richmond: The Dietz Press, 1944).

Pollard, Edward A., *Southern History of the War: The Third Year of the War* (New York: Charles B. Richardson, 1863).

Hutchins, E. R., *The War of the Sixties* (New York: The Beale Publishing Company, 1912).

CPSIA information can be obtained
at www.ICGtesting.com
Printed in the USA
LVHW022112030423
743361LV00034B/1612